a place for the words
I'll never say

Ariana Alessandri

a place for the words I'll never say © 2022
Ariana Alessandri

All rights reserved.

No part of this publication may be
reproduced, stored in a retrieval system, or
transmitted, in any form or by any means,
electronic, mechanical, photocopying,
recording or otherwise, without the prior
written permission of the presenters.

Ariana Alessandri asserts the moral right to
be identified as author of this work.

Presentation by *BookLeaf Publishing*

Web: www.bookleafpub.com

E-mail: info@bookleafpub.com

ISBN : 9789357699198

First edition 2022

DEDICATION

To my parents,

who have always encouraged me to write.

And to MJR,

who made me believe that love is real.

PREFACE

I began writing poems consistently as I processed the worst heartbreak of my life. I continued writing as I found that new love comes with its own challenges. Insecurity, regret, reflection, and growth are all parts of my journey.

Here is a collection of poems that express the emotions that I'm often too afraid to say out loud.

Hurricane

She is a walking contradiction -
one part beauty, two parts chaos

there's a fire in her eyes,
a rhythm to her step,
wind in her hair

nobody sees
the broken bones beneath her jeans
the bullets in her lungs
the scars etched deep into her heart

despite the pain,
she is a hurricane
and nothing in this world
could stop her.

Promise

I know you're hurting

I know your heart
is split in two
like part of your soul is crumbling
your limbs to ashes

this feeling will pass

the memories will fade
and one day soon
you'll be able to smile again
one day soon
you'll be able to look in a mirror
and see a girl
who did what she
once deemed impossible:
heal

she will have healed her heart
mind and soul
so that she'll be free
to find happiness again

I know you're hurting right now
but I promise
it's not forever.

Circumstance

You don't miss him

what you miss
is your projected fantasy
of what could have
should have
or would have been
had the circumstances been different.

Confusion

I know you have grown accustomed
to being torn apart inside
but do not confuse love
with simply
the lack of heartache.

Brave

Other girls are brave

they can open themselves up
like flowers in bloom,
and share their souls
with anyone
who cares enough
to give them water
and sunlight

she is not brave

if she were a flower,
she would come with thorns
and if a man ever wished
her petals open
he would need to place
in her hands
the ocean
and the sun itself.

Guarantee

If I give you all of me
where is my guarantee
that it will be enough?

She

She is completely
unaware
of the power
she holds over you

her smile alone
is like the sunrise
warm and bright
her laughter is music
to your ears
and her words
are your favorite lullaby

the way she looks at you,
with a mischievous twinkle
in her dark eyes
awakens something inside of you
that hasn't been stirred before

she is innocent but clever
wise but carefree
open but a challenge

she is the kind of woman
you have been waiting for.

Insecurity

I wish I could take back
the hours I've wasted
in front of the mirror
ripping apart
every inch of my body,
the workings of my mind,
the composition of my soul

I've created an idol of a ghost
and gave her a name,
a name you used to love

she is everything that I am not

I'm afraid that I won't measure up
that my features are dull,
my humor is dry,
and my heart is weak
by comparison

most of all
I'm afraid that if
I let myself think
for just one moment
that I am worth it
I will discover
that I'm not

my constant reminder is this:

if even she
wasn't worth it to you
what hope do I have?

New

I don't want to love like you
I don't want to move like you
I don't want to touch like you
I don't want to taste like you
I don't want to trust like you
I don't want to break like you

I don't want to fill your shoes
I'm somebody new.

Regret

Do not punish him
for a past he isn't proud of
when all he truly wants
is a future
with you.

Man

You showed me an old picture of yourself
and I couldn't help but think,
"there is a boy who another girl loved"

there is a boy who another girl
thought was charming
funny
interesting

there is a boy who another girl
laughed with
cried with
grew up with

there is a boy
who was loved by a girl
who wasn't me

but when I think of you now
I don't think of the boy in the photo
I don't think of a boy at all

everything about you is different
from the wrinkles around your eyes when you
smile
to the fullness in your shoulders,
in your voice, in your presence

to the way that you think, act, and reason

everything about you has changed

the only thing
you have in common
with the boy in the photo
are distant memories

you were a boy
who another girl loved

but you aren't a boy
anymore.

Last

But who is to say
that your first
and your last
cannot be the one and the same?

Ocean

Crash into me
like a wave against the shore
pull me under
until you drown out
my fears, worries, and doubts

fill my senses
with your sight, sound, taste, and touch
until I'm lost in you
like I'm lost at sea
only I don't want to be found
I want to be taken
to be swept away…
but I'm still afraid of the water

only you
can teach me
how to swim.

Remember

Remember
your story is written
by the painter of the sky.

Music

Your fingers dance across my skin,
like they dance across piano keys

you play me like a song
it's soft at first
gentile
careful
quiet

but it grows louder
wilder
more eager
with every note

we are lost in the melody
the harmony
the synchronicity
until the crescendo
unravels us both

our souls make music
out of love.

Inside

Please understand
when my body is against yours
my heart and soul
are inside you too.

Words

There are ways to say
"I love you"
without words

a gentle nudge
a warm glance
a sweet smile
a brush of your lips against my cheek
or your fingers across my palm

these are the ways we say
"I love you"
without words.

Fall

We don't step into love
we don't walk, jog, or even run

we fall

we fall freely, without reservation
praying only that something
or someone
will be there to catch us

I have fallen for you
over and over again
faster and further
than each time before

when I fall apart in your arms,
you piece me back together
with gentle words
and soft kisses
until I am whole again

and when we fall together
it feels like flying
like the most exciting thing
I've ever known
is being yours

so I will keep falling
even if I might get hurt
even if it might be scary
even if I don't have all the answers

I don't need all the answers

I trust that
I will always land safely
in your arms.

Desire

I'm screaming through
my fingertips
as you taste
desire
on my lips

I'm terrified
of letting myself slip

I didn't know
it would feel
like this
that my own body
could betray
my will

how can a man
be so hard to resist?

Unity

Every so often
I confuse your hands with mine
like you are an extension of me
or I am an extension of you
we are one and the same
two bodies
one soul.

Live

Smile as much as you breathe
laugh as much as you speak
dance whenever you hear music
find shapes in the clouds
admire the sunrise
dare to dream
tell people what they mean to you
don't be afraid of failure
forgive those who have hurt you
and love like you've never been broken.

www.ingramcontent.com/pod-product-compliance
Lightning Source LLC
LaVergne TN
LVHW021355200726

843509LV00014B/2865